REVOLUTIO

Ten Principles
That Will Empower
to Change the Worl

by **David Pierce**
with Aaron Pierce and Benjamin Pierce

steiger international press

Revolutionary! Ten Principles That Will Empower Christian Artists to Change the World
by David Pierce
with Aaron Pierce and Benjamin Pierce

Second, revised edition

First published in 2013.
This edition published in 2017.

All sources for the quotes used in this book can be found at the end of the book.

Cover design by Steiger Design Office, Krögis
Published and distributed by

Steiger International
PO Box 480
Huntington, MA 01050
U.S.A.

Order by
Email: intoffice@steiger.org
Website: www.steiger.org

ISBN 978-0-473-23873-5

FOR THE LOST

Acknowledgements

This book would not be possible without the hard work of many dedicated people. To my beautiful wife Jodi who keeps me sane. To my sons, Aaron and Benjamin, for the privilege and joy of working on this book with you. To Nicci Hubert, Susan Bradley, David Donnelly, Steven Bradley, Mary Nichols, Celinda Sorenson, Molly Waggoner, Jennifer Pierce and Stuart Bennett for your valuable input. This book is stronger because of your contribution.
Finally, to Felipe Rocha and Cristian Faber for your hard work on the design.

I was in Nashville, Tennessee, speaking to some of the biggest Christian bands and major record label representatives in the industry. I told them that God has a heart for the lost and encouraged them to use the huge platform they had been given to proclaim the truth to people who have only heard lies. I challenged them that they could go anywhere and speak boldly about Jesus, because there are no closed doors for Him.

Afterward, a musician who had just signed a major record deal came to me and said, "When we started our band, we were going to secular clubs and telling people about Jesus. We really felt that it was something God wanted us to do. But now we have signed this record deal, so we have to do the Christian club circuit. We have to play in all these Christian venues, and we kind of feel like we've sold out." He was looking for me to tell him that it was okay, but all I could do was look back at him and say, "Yes, you've sold out."

INTRODUCTION

> "I am convinced that the potential of reaching people for Jesus through the media—whether it be records, radio, movies, or television—is monumental, simply because these are the things that have, and continue to hold, people's attention. I truly believe that Christians who are completely sold out to God, using these tools, can bring people to their knees in repentance and lead them into the waiting arms of the Savior."
>
> Keith Green[1]

INTRODUCTION

In 2011, I was in Beirut, Lebanon, with my wife, Jodi. We were in a television studio in the center of the city preparing for my second interview on MTV Lebanon.

I had been invited by Imad, a man who, according to many, brought rock music to the Middle East and is the C.O.O. of the multimedia and broadcasting conglomerate that owns MTV Lebanon.

We first met in 2008 when he came with one of his daughters to see our band, No Longer Music, perform in the center of Beirut. After that show, I was able to pray with his daughter and him, and since then we have become friends.

In 2010, he invited me back to Beirut to do my first interview on MTV Lebanon. I was able to talk openly about Jesus in a part of the world where the Gospel is rarely heard. Surprisingly, it was so well received that Imad was open to having me come back for a second interview a year later.

During my 2011 interview, Imad and I agreed that I would talk about "Jesus, rock and roll, and power," and that I would explain that Jesus is about love, not hate. This is an important message in a part of the world where Christianity is associated with hatred and violence.

I went on to say that Jesus was not just another prophet or teacher—an incredibly radical statement in the Muslim world. I added, "Because he came back to life, the death sentence in my life can be broken."

This interview was broadcasted in Arabic all over the Middle East. Afterward, I called Imad to thank him for letting me come, and he told me that I was "always welcome back and that Lebanon was open to us."

This opportunity really was nothing short of a miracle when you consider how plainly I was able to present Jesus. Who else but God could open up this door for me?

In 2012, I returned to Beirut and was able to openly proclaim the Gospel during live interviews on MTV, OTV, and SAT-7, which were broadcasted to millions all over the Middle East.

You see, God desires to show His power outside the church. He is looking for men and women who are not going to be satisfied to just see His power within the context of church culture, but who are willing to do what it takes to see Him move in secular places.

I could write book after book filled with examples of how I've seen God move outside of the church. I've seen hardened gang members fall to their knees, weeping and repenting of their sins after an open-air concert in Jamaica. I've seen God's power fall so strongly in "First Avenue," a prominent club made famous by Prince in Minneapolis, Minnesota (USA), that the bartender couldn't work because he was shaking so much.

People today need to see the real Jesus, because there is power when He is proclaimed. I can testify that if you are willing to step outside the Christian "ghetto" and boldly proclaim the message of Christ, He will move in ways that will astound you. Here's another example: I was in Santiago, Chile, with my band, No Longer Music. We were playing in a famous Chilean club, and the place was filled with people doing hard drugs. There was vomit everywhere, even on stage. The bathrooms were in such bad condition that you could hardly use them. The singer of the opening band had been drinking and had done so much speed that after his performance he collapsed in the hallway backstage. As we performed, the audience began to realize that we were singing about Jesus. They started screaming, swearing, and giving us the finger. The club owner even put a pornographic video on the TV behind the bar.

I discovered after the concert that even though we experienced all sorts of opposition, God's power was still evident. One guy, trying to describe his experience to me, said, "When you were speaking, I felt a life force coming from you."

The next day, we played in a warehouse. I had invited someone from a local church to come and translate my preaching after the concert. But before my translator could translate, Cocke, the guitarist from the well-known Chilean metal band we were touring with, started translating from the sound desk even though he was not a Christian. He passionately translated my words into Spanish and told the people in the club that Jesus was the answer.

Afterwards, I asked Cocke why he translated my preaching. He told me that when I started to preach, he started sweating and shaking and that the words were forced out of his mouth. A few days later, Cocke came to a meeting at a local church and fell to his knees and gave his life to Jesus. He saw that Jesus is not just talk but is powerful, and it was worth surrendering his life to Him. Since then, Cocke's life has been totally transformed, and God has given him the heart of a radical evangelist.

On another tour, in São Paulo, Brazil, a guy who ran a male strip joint offered us the use of one of his clubs for a follow-up meeting. We thought it would be ideal, since the people who saw our concerts at hard-core gothic clubs would never have come to a Christian venue. We started our meeting by playing some normal worship music. While we were playing, the guy who organized strippers for the club was on the phone in his basement office. He came upstairs a few minutes later and told me, "I heard your music upstairs, and a power came into my office, and the mirror on the wall exploded." He took me down to where he had been working. Broken glass was scattered everywhere. He said, "I understand that it's not just the glass that is breaking, but that something is also breaking inside of me." Then this tough guy, covered in tattoos, collapsed in my arms and wept like a baby, because he felt the power of Jesus.

"There are Christian artists who seem more full of art than Christ and at times it would perhaps take God Himself to understand the meaning of their excellent, creative lyrics."

Glenn Kaiser[2]

PLATFORM

> "The Church exists for nothing else but to draw men into Christ, to make them little Christs. If they are not doing that, all the cathedrals, clergy, missions, sermons, even the Bible itself, are simply a waste of time. God became Man for no other purpose."
>
> C.S. Lewis[3]

PLATFORM

The first few years of my ministry were not spent on a stage, but on the streets and in the clubs of Amsterdam. I felt like God wanted me to take time to get to know people who were alienated from the church. So for two years I did nothing but go into the clubs, talk to people, ask questions, and listen. I wrote down the names of people I met and spent hours praying that God would give me His heart for them and that He would touch their lives with His power. It was during this time that God started giving me His heart for the lost.

It was out of a love for people that God called me to start a band and use it as a tool to reach the lost by bringing the message of Jesus to where they are, in their own context, as modeled by the example and teaching of Jesus.

Jesus ultimately was motivated out of love. In Matthew 9:36, it says Jesus had compassion on the multitudes because "they were confused and helpless, like sheep without a shepherd." No one would argue that we live in a world that desperately needs to hear the truth. If we truly love people, as Jesus loves people, wouldn't we want to use every platform God gives to share the truth with them? It comes down to what motivates you in your art. Does a love for Jesus and a heart for the lost drive you to share the truth, or has the art become an idol?

I believe art is a gift from God, and our creativity is an expression of how we are made in God's image. Art can be used in worship, for pleasure, and even as a way to earn a living. However, I believe if we truly love people, we will want them to know the truth. As an artist, I certainly enjoy the process of producing art, but I've seen time and time again how God can use art to transform broken lives. This is my greatest motivation as an artist.

Sadly, very few Christian artists are using their art as a tool to reach the lost. It seems that nowadays, so many Christians are entering the art scene only to perform for other Christians. And those who perform for secular audiences choose not to share Jesus through their art in a clear way, if at all.

I often hear bands say, "We are not an evangelistic band. Don't lay this burden on us, saying we have to be telling people about Jesus. We are just musicians who happen to be followers of Jesus."

Can you imagine an anarchistic band ever saying, "We're not an anarchistic band; we're just a band made up of anarchists. We don't want to push anarchy on people. We just want people to see anarchy in our lives." If everyone else can speak clearly without restraint, why is it that so many Christians feel like they have to keep silent, especially when there is so much authority in their message?

The world is a desperate place and millions of people are being destroyed by the lies of Satan, spread by the entertainment industry, the music industry, and a global pop culture that preys on people. Wouldn't God desire his name to be lifted up in these places?

Ultimately, it is an issue of the heart. What is the purpose of your art? We are called to serve God with everything we have, and this should include our art.

I believe that God's heart is broken because far too often, those in the church who have received artistic gifts from Him are unwilling to boldly proclaim the truth outside the church.

It's true; some may be called to make a living with their art. Yet regardless of our vocation, we are all called to be witnesses for Christ. In the end we will all be held accountable for how we used the platform we were given. Did we use our time, energy and talent for God's purposes and His glory, or for ourselves?

We have to realize that most people in the world are trying to find out where their next meal will come from. And here we are, so rich that we can spend our time creating art. And not only that, but this luxury also gives us a platform to have influence over many people.

Jesus is looking for artists who are willing to tell people the truth. Romans 10:14 says, "How can they call on the one they have not believed in? And how can they believe in the one of whom they have not heard? And how can they hear without someone preaching to them?"

One night, we were playing in a jazz club in Bishkek, Kyrgyzstan. Many of the musical elite from the city were there, and a television crew came to do an interview and film our show. After the concert, the art director asked if she could talk with me. "Don't translate the next show," she said. "It's good art by itself, and it doesn't need translation."

I knew that she was saying this to me because some people in the audience were offended by the clear message we were bringing about Jesus. So I said to her, "Most people liked what they saw, right?"

"Yes," she admitted.

"So it's only a few people, then, who don't like our message?"

Again, she said, "Yes."

"So then, why are you letting those fascists tell you what to do?" I asked. "Good art is confrontational. It is supposed to be provocative, and I want to be provocative. I'm not interested in doing something that's going to put people to sleep."

So she said, "You're right."

We were allowed to translate the next show. After the concert, she gave her life to Jesus.

So the question is, if there is so much authority in the message of Christ, why do Christian artists still hide it? I have a theory: it's because when you talk about Jesus, you enter into a battle.

One time, we were in an Arab town in southern Turkey, near the Syrian border. There was no Christian presence in the area; it was populated entirely by Muslims. The beach was littered with broken glass, garbage, and dead rats. We felt a really dark spirit as we began to set up our equipment to do our concert on the main road, which was covered with garbage just like the beach. I helped to unload the gear, and then went for a walk to invite people to the concert. Everyone I talked to was friendly. After I had given out all the fliers I had, I started to head back to the street where the band was setting up. As I was walking, I saw a tough-looking, twenty-something guy coming toward me.

I thought to myself, this guy looks like he would be perfect to invite to our concert. So I said hello and then pointed to where we were setting up, and said, "You need to come to our concert. You will really like it." But as I said this, he punched my chest and shoved me up against a wall. I tried to walk away, but he wouldn't let me go. Instead, he pulled out a long, thin knife shaped like a needle (I have since learned that it is called an assassin's knife). I put out my hands and said, "Sorry," and then tried to explain that I was only inviting him to our concert. He sinisterly repeated my words, shouting, "Sorry! Sorry!" and then pulled back his knife to stab me. Fortunately, a guy standing nearby shouted something to him, and he just stopped and walked away.

This happened just before our concert, and I didn't want to bring fear into the band, so I didn't tell them what happened. But I couldn't shield them from other difficulties. Throughout the entire show a strong wind blew, covering everything in sand and making it nearly impossible to keep our set upright.

Despite the conditions, God gave me an amazing spirit of freedom to preach plainly and boldly about Jesus before the hundreds of people who surrounded us on all sides.

After the concert, the band members spent several hours in conversations talking to people about Jesus. I prayed with three young men whose faces were literally glowing because God's presence was so strong upon them. They thanked us profusely and gave us their contact details so that they could take part in a Bible correspondence course. The response was incredible. A local missionary believed that in this particular region the Gospel had not been openly preached for more than a thousand years. But it was not only a historic event, it was also a huge miracle, because in this Arab town, 200 people were so moved by God's power that they prayed out loud and said that they wanted to follow Jesus.

I have been in a lot of crazy situations because of our band's commitment to speak clearly about Jesus. We have played concerts where people spat all over us. One time our sound guy was hit in the face with a lit cigarette. Another time, he had to wrestle with the owner of a club who wanted to turn off my microphone while I was speaking. I've been laughed at. I've been in concerts where no one clapped, but no one would leave either. At one concert, somebody threw a bottle at my head; it missed me but hit our drummer and cut his leg. We have been banned from playing in clubs because of our message. We have been a big joke because we talk about Jesus.

One time, we played in a club in New Zealand, and two other Christian bands played before us. Even though they were Christians, they didn't really talk about Jesus, so everybody in the club really liked them. When it was our turn, on the other hand, they quickly discovered who we were and what we were talking about. The club owner passed me a note that said, "Shut down your set." We had to just stop in the middle of our show.

I went out into the parking lot and started thinking, God, maybe I'm just too hard-core about this whole thing. I mean, look at these other bands; everybody in the club loved them. And then they shut down our set. Am I making a mistake here? Wouldn't it be better if we were more subtle, if we just played music? Wouldn't that be better?

And as I was praying, I felt like God spoke to me and said, "Are you going to be ashamed of the cross? Are you going to be ashamed of me?" So I said, "Okay, God, I am not going to deny you. Even if we never get another invitation to play again; I am going to tell people the truth."

It is about giving up control of your life. Jesus said, "Whoever wants to save their life will lose it, but whoever loses their life for me will find it" (Matthew 16:25). So whether you are a CEO of a major company or an artist, Jesus calls you to surrender and obey Him.

Many Christian artists say they want to be radical for Jesus, but they follow the same set of rules as the world. If you truly want to be "radical" in a way that will allow you to see God's power, you are going to have to go against conventional wisdom. It begins with the understanding that the art is not your motivation, and that is completely different from how the world approaches it. It is also completely different from how most Christians approach it.

Most people say something like, "God has gifted me to be a guitarist, and I love music, so I want to play music for God. I want to look for opportunities to express myself, and I like certain kinds of music, so I am going to play the kind of music that I enjoy. And this is the group of people that I feel the most comfortable with, so that is the group of people that I will be involved with."

However, if we are following Jesus, it's not about our likes or dislikes, it is about God's call on our lives. That means that He decides what kind of music we play or art we make, and He decides what kind of people we go to. This is a completely different way of looking at it.

For example, when I started out, God told me that he wanted me to reach the punks and anarchists in Amsterdam, but that was not a cool thing for me. I had absolutely no attraction to that culture. I didn't like the music, I didn't like the scene, and I didn't like going to the clubs. There was nothing about it that attracted me, but I knew God had called me to reach them. Was I going to be obedient? Was I willing to surrender my plans and receive God's plans for my life?

Ultimately, my band, No Longer Music, came out of complete surrender to God's plans. Sadly, too many Christian artists approach things differently, saying, "God, I want to do this, so bless it." But the way I believe we should approach our lives and talents is to say, "God, I surrender everything to you. Tell me what you want me to do."

In this book, I have outlined ten principles that I have learned from over 30 years of bringing the message of Jesus into secular places around the world using music and other forms of art.

I primarily use music, visual art, and theater to illustrate the principles that I talk about in this book because this is the area I have been intimately involved in. However, I believe the principles that are outlined in this book apply to other forms of art as well and to followers of Jesus in general.

If you are willing to surrender your plan for God's plan and apply these principles to your art, you will enter into the revolutionary life you were created for.

Responding to This Material

1. Take a few moments to write down an honest assessment of your core motivation for doing art. What is driving you?

2. Have you encountered opposition in sharing Christ through your art? How have you responded?

3. Discuss or reflect on this point: "Good art is confrontational. It is supposed to be provocative, and I want to be provocative. I'm not interested in doing something that's going to put people to sleep."

4. Assess your willingness to surrender your plans and dreams for those that God would have for you.

5. Memorize and meditate on Romans 10:14 and Matthew 16:25.

"Prayer pulls the rope down below and the great bell rings above in the ears of God. Some scarcely stir the bell, for they pray so languidly; others give only an occasional jerk at the rope. But he who communicates with heaven is the man who grasps the rope boldly and pulls continuously with all his might."

C.H. Spurgeon[4]

PRINCIPLE 1:
God Rewards Those Who Seek Him with a Desperate Heart

> "... without faith it is impossible to please God, because anyone who comes to him must believe that he exists and that he rewards those who earnestly seek him."
>
> Hebrews 11:6

PRINCIPLE 1: God Rewards Those Who Seek Him with a Desperate Heart

There are millions of talented musicians and artists. What the world needs is not more great artists; the world needs Jesus. If you are called to have an impact in the secular world—as I believe many readers of this book are—the key is knowing Jesus.

Yes, you should strive to make the best art possible. However, so many Christian artists who started out wanting to make a difference for God end up chasing after the same thing that secular artists do. They devote all their time to artistic excellence and believe somehow that this is the key to having an impact for God.

Glenn Kaiser, a famous Christian artist in the 1970s, said that "trying to impress the ungodly by artistic excellence—though God desires our offerings to be excellent—is a trap and a folly."[5]

We must recognize that it is not the quality of our art that gives us power and authority, it is God. The problem with most Christian artists is that they are too focused on the art.

I think the typical Christian band figures, we should pray before we rehearse. So they pray, "Jesus, help us to have a good practice!" And then they practice for hours. Afterwards they might say, "Thank you, Jesus, for giving us a good practice."

But is this truly seeking God, or is it just paying him lip service? We should approach God with the same passion and intensity with which we approach our art. Cry out to him, spend all night in prayer, go for long prayer walks, ask God to take your art and fill it with His power. Don't limit Him; seek wholeheartedly what He wants. Pray as much as you paint, or write, or film, or practice. If more Christian artists would do this, it would revolutionize the Christian art scene.

What if for every hour you practice your art, you spent an hour or more seeking God? It would revolutionize everything!

I'm often asked how my band, No Longer Music, gets so many invitations to play around the world. People want to know our promotional strategy, but I tell them when God is behind you, you do not need the promotional tools or the financial backing that the world says you need. Bands do not even need CDs. They don't need a promo pack. They don't need a record label. If God is behind you, you simply do not need that stuff.

No Longer Music has been playing in clubs, bars, and secular musical festivals on countless tours all over the world for over 25 years, not because of marketing or promotion but because God opens doors for those who seek Him. I don't believe it is bad for Christian artists to use promotional tools to market themselves, I am simply suggesting if they would trust God and seek Him, He would open doors that would far surpass what would ordinarily be possible.

I was walking on the beach in front of my house one day and for some reason I was thinking about Brazil. I said to God, "I would love for my band to do something in Brazil." When I got home, I had received an e-mail from a guy named Sandro Baggio in São Paulo. It said, "I heard you are coming to Brazil; can I set up a tour for you?" God had put Brazil on my heart and without promotion or even a contact in that country, God opened the door to not only go to Brazil but eventually other South American countries as well. Seek God and He will give you the opportunities!

Later I started thinking about the Middle East. Again, I started praying. "God, I would love to do something in the Middle East. I would love to see Your power there." Once again, I checked my e-mail. David Wilson, a concert organizer based in Istanbul, Turkey, had written me saying, "I set up concert tours in the Middle East. Can I set something up for you? Tell me where you want to go, and I will set up a tour."

If God is behind you, He will open up the doors. Nothing will be impossible. And God loves it when we seek Him. He loves it when we cry out to Him. And He rewards those who seek Him with a desperate heart.

When you make knowing God the priority, you will feel incredibly free because you won't feel bound by worldly obstacles.

One time, we went to a club where we had been invited to play, but when the manager saw us, he shut the door in our faces, saying, "Forget about it, there's no way you can play here." For some reason, I didn't feel like leaving. So we just sat in the parking lot in front of the club and prayed. We didn't bug him or ask him if we could stay, but we didn't leave either, we just sat and prayed that God would open the door for us to play in the club. Finally, after a couple hours, the manager came back out and said, "All right, all right, you can play," and let us in. We had a great concert, and people gave their lives to Jesus that night.

The spiritual battles that we encounter as we enter secular places are intense. That is another reason why I believe strongly that intense spiritual preparation is absolutely essential—it is the reason we see God come in such great power on our tours. The more we seek God, the more His power will be demonstrated through our ministry as we go to secular places. That is why I continue to make spiritual preparation an absolute priority.

During our rehearsals prior to our tours, we spend at least an hour studying the Bible and in prayer every day before we begin. Often, we will get away for a time of solitude in a secluded area to bathe ourselves in God's presence.

Throughout the tour itself, we spend time praying every day collectively as a group and individually. Sometimes, I sense that what we are doing is so intense that we need to start a 24-hour prayer chain among the band members. Normally, two people pray for an hour at a time and then wake up the next two people. This is not dead, dry prayer time; these are exciting times with God. Sometimes the band gets so into it that they pray beyond their shift because it is energizing and exhilarating to seek God and then see Him move in real ways the next day.

2 Chronicles 16:9 says that "the eyes of the Lord search the whole earth in order to strengthen those whose hearts are fully committed to Him." God

desires to use you to change the world, but it's only going to happen if you earnestly seek Him. Yes, make the best art possible, but good art is not going to change the world; only God's power will. If you seek God desperately and look to Him for opportunities, there is no limit to the impact He can have through your art!

Responding to This Material

1. What are the implications of the promise in Hebrews 11:6 as it relates to your art?

2. Evaluate your prayer life. If the impact of your art and its message were based solely on the quality of your prayer life, what results would you anticipate?

3. Do an audit of how you spend your time. Compare the hours spent working on your art versus the hours seeking God (prayer and word).

4. Discuss or reflect on this point: "The quality of our art is not the source of opportunities, God is."

5. Honestly evaluate what you see as the source of opportunities. Where do you place your trust?

6. Memorize and meditate on Hebrews 11:6 and 2 Chronicles 16:9.

PRINCIPLE 2:
Audience of One

> "Whatever you do, work at it with all your heart, as working for the Lord, not for human masters, since you know that you will receive an inheritance from the Lord as a reward. It is the Lord Christ you are serving."
>
> Colossians 3:23-24

PRINCIPLE 2: Audience of One

Over the years I have had virtually every kind of experience imaginable as an artist. I have played for packed halls and empty clubs. I have played on big stages with top-of-the-line equipment and on the ground with equipment that barely worked. I have learned that with God there is no wasted opportunity. He uses everything for His purposes.

One time we were invited to play at a large festival in Brazil. The local bands were afraid that we would take people away from their shows because we were an international act, so they insisted that we play first. The venue could hold around 5,000 people, but it was totally empty when we were told to play. Because we were opening the festival, nobody was there when we started. So backstage I told the band that we needed to play with more intensity than if it was a packed house because this show was going to be just for Jesus. He was our audience and we would give Him our best. In a totally empty auditorium we did the whole show with everything we had and it was great.

There are times when God wants to remind us that we are really performing for an audience of one.

Of course I love to play in front of large crowds, but ultimately everything I do is first and foremost an act of worship to God alone.

God has given me moments throughout the years that remind me that He is in charge. There is freedom in knowing that He is in control of the size of the crowd. What God asks of us is to offer all we have to Him and leave the results in His hands. There are no wasted moments. Our concert in Brazil was worship to God. I think God will bring moments in your life that will test whether or not you are willing to play for an audience of one!

As noted above, Paul says it this way in Colossians 3:23-24: "Whatever you do, work at it with all your heart, as working for the Lord, not for human masters, since you know that you will receive an inheritance from the Lord as a reward. It is the Lord Christ you are serving."

Playing for an audience of one means starting with what God gives you. When my band first started, our equipment wasn't impressive, but we were happy to have it. We often played in small clubs for small crowds, but again we were grateful for the opportunities that God gave us.

As I reflect on our humble beginning, I believe God was seeing if we would be faithful. Even with bad equipment, a handful of songs, and only a few people watching, would we give it everything? When God saw that we were faithful with little, He began to trust us with more.

Starting with what you have means being willing to play wherever God provides the opportunity and not denying Him even if the only person watching is the janitor cleaning the club. It also means giving one hundred percent of your effort in every show, whether it's in front of twenty people or a thousand.

Do I prepare diligently if I know it's going to be a small crowd? Do I pray with the same intensity?

You don't know how God might use a seemingly insignificant moment. My prayers, effort, and preparation should be the same regardless of the size of the audience. You don't know why God has you there. He may have purposes that you don't see, or He may be preparing you for greater opportunities in the future.

I was invited to speak at one of the largest Christian festivals in the U.S. There were hundreds of thousands of people at the outdoor stages, but I was put in a small indoor stage that was organized by some high school kids. As I arrived, the emcee mistakenly announced to the crowd that there would be no speaker even though I was on the schedule. So the relatively small crowd headed for the exits, leaving only a handful of people standing in the back as I got up to speak. Everything inside of me just wanted to leave. What was I doing speaking in this lame little tent? But this was a test. I chose to preach with the same intensity I would have used on one of the main stages outside speaking to thousands. I preached before an audience of one.

Not long after that, God provided my first interview opportunity on MTV Lebanon, which was broadcast to millions all over the Arab world. I think God wanted to see if I would be faithful with a "small" thing before He would give me a "big" thing.

Of course God can use artists who play in front of big crowds and have great equipment. The crowd and the equipment are not the point; it's about the heart. Are you willing to serve God in small ways with less-than-perfect equipment when no one is watching? God will use the small moments in our lives to shape our character so that He can use us in greater ways in the future.

God will use some seemingly insignificant experiences to build your faith. In 1 Samuel 17:32-37, David offers to fight Goliath. Saul and his men laugh at him, but notice David's response to Saul: "Your servant has been keeping his father's sheep. When a lion or a bear came and carried off a sheep from the flock, I went after it, struck it and rescued the sheep from its mouth. When it turned on me, I seized it by its hair, struck it and killed it. Your servant has killed both the lion and the bear; this uncircumcised Philistine will be like one of them, because he has defied the armies of the living God. The LORD who rescued me from the paw of the lion and the paw of the bear will rescue me from the hand of this Philistine."

David experienced God's faithfulness when he faced the lion and the bear, and God used this experience to build his faith so he was ready to face Goliath.

In the early days of our ministry, God used small victories to build my faith and prepare me to take bigger steps in the future. I was able to trust God in big battles because I had seen His victory in small ones.

At its core, playing for an audience of one is about your motivation. If you are motivated to glorify God through your art, then regardless of the size of crowd, quality of the equipment, or significance of the opportunity, you will give it everything you have. There won't be wasted opportunities because you will see every circumstance as worship to God and trust that He is shaping your character or building your faith.

Serving God through art can be a difficult challenge. It's very easy to become discouraged. Keeping my focus on performing for an audience of one has helped me persevere and stay true to what God has called me to do.

Responding to This Material

1. How does performing for an “audience of one” impact your motivation and attitude about your art?

2. Discuss or reflect on this point: “God wanted to see if I would be faithful with the ‘small’ thing before He would give me the ‘big’ thing.”

3. Are your prayers, effort, and preparation the same regardless of the size of the audience?

4. How has God used seemingly insignificant experiences in your life to build your faith?

5. Memorize and meditate on Colossians 3:23-24.

PRINCIPLE 3:
God Wants the Glory

> "Glorifying the only worthy One has to be a minister's most important goal!"
>
> Keith Green[6]

PRINCIPLE 3: God Wants the Glory

It's important to ask the question, who is getting credit for your art? I often think I am serving God, but in reality I am just trying to make a name for myself. But God wants to get the glory for what I do.

Shortly after I started No Longer Music, we got an invitation to play on a talk show in Holland. It is called Sonja on Monday, and at that time it was one of the most famous talk shows in Holland. It would be like playing on the Late Show with David Letterman, except that it broadcasts live. I was excited to play because I thought that God was going to use this opportunity to open up many doors. I felt like we played well and the studio audience seemed to enjoy it. After the show, I asked a few friends who had watched us on TV how they thought we did, but they kept changing the subject.

I went back to our apartment, and in the mailbox there was a note saying, "David, did you know that you sang out of tune?"

After that, I would walk down the street and people would recognize me and start laughing. I would go to a grocery store, and they would say, "Didn't we see you on Sonja?" And they would mock me.

I needed some peace, so I went to the zoo. I was sitting at an outdoor café trying to collect my thoughts, and even there people laughed at me. I remember crying out to God asking him why this had happened. "Why did you allow me to sing poorly?"

I was frustrated because I honestly felt like my heart was in the right place and that, deep down, my desire was to give God the glory. I believed that if we played well, it would give us many opportunities to tell people about Jesus, and yet I sang out of tune. Again, I asked God why He allowed this to happen and I felt like God said, "I allowed you to sing badly so that when I use your band, everyone will know it is because of Me, not your singing."

God wants to get the glory for what I do. Fortunately I do not sing out of tune very often, but this was a key moment for me as an artist. God allowed this to happen to remind me that great talent and a perfect performance, while not wrong in themselves, can get in the way of God getting the glory. I want to perform well and my band works very hard, but ultimately God made it very clear during that time that if my art was going to have a significant impact, it could not be about me. So I challenge you, regardless of how much talent God has given you, to give Him the glory. Human praise is cheap and it is a poor substitute for the amazing impact your art can have if you give God the credit.

When God does give us a greater platform with our art, we have a responsibility to give Him the glory. One time, No Longer Music was invited to play on the main stage of a major festival in Europe in front of an audience of 15,000 people. At that point many Christians started telling me, "Don't say anything about Jesus. This is an amazing opportunity. Don't blow it. God has given you this opportunity, so be cool; just play your music." I began asking God how I should handle this situation, and He reminded me of a U2 concert Jodi and I had attended many years earlier.

We all stood on our chairs, hanging on Bono's every word, and it was a surreal experience. I had heard that Bono was a Christian and kept waiting for him to give God the glory, but he never did. And everyone left the stadium singing, "I still haven't found what I am looking for."

I remember leaving the concert and saying, "Jesus, I know I'm not a great artist like Bono, but if you ever give me an opportunity like this, I will give you the glory." Years later, God reminded me of what I promised Him that day as I was preparing for this major festival in Europe. So I said to God, "Okay, even if this ends all of our opportunities, I am going to do what I promised. I am going to give you the glory." So despite the opposition, I preached.

The concert went really well, and even after I preached, the crowd kept calling us back for encores. After the third encore, the organizers said, "This is messing up the whole festival." The audience was going crazy, because they wanted us to keep coming back on the stage. I believe God anointed us that night because we were willing to be bold even if it meant looking foolish and risking future opportunities. We gave God the glory and the opportunities only continued to increase, but this only came by being willing to risk it all.

God will test your heart. Every artist who wants to make a radical difference for Jesus needs to come to the point where giving God the glory is non-negotiable even if it means never getting another opportunity again. Giving God the credit for success is a struggle for artists because they are so cool. It doesn't matter how small the venue, gallery, or audience; those in the art scene are unbearably cool. Bands on the same bill will rarely talk to each other. Artists and musicians can be some of the most critical and judgmental people you will meet. This spirit of 'coolness,' sadly, exists among Christian artists and bands as well.

God is strongly opposed to pride (James 4:6), and that's all this is—pride. As Christian artists, we need to practice uncoolness. What I mean by this is you need to actively fight the pride you can so easily take on as an artist. I know because I have been guilty of this myself. But don't let it suck you in. Talk to other bands, be in the front row of their concert, be encouraging, and don't take yourself so seriously! How do we expect to reach the music scene, which includes other bands, when we are critical and judgmental like everyone else? We need to practice uncoolness!

There was a time when Christians would wear "What Would Jesus Do?" wristbands. Normally, I wouldn't be into wearing one. They just aren't my thing. But one time, I was speaking at a church, and someone came up to me, put one on my wrist, and said, "I want you to have this." I thought, "Well, that's nice and I appreciate the gesture, but it really isn't my thing," and I planned to cut it off when I got out into the parking lot. But then I felt like God said to me, "Are you so cool that you can't wear a "What Would Jesus Do?" bracelet? You wear that bracelet! I don't care if it's not your style. You wear it anyway." So I wore that bracelet until it rotted off my wrist several years later.

I am telling you, be uncool. Fight against pride. Go against it. If you are called to the music scene, you are called to an incredibly arrogant and proud world. The more you are willing to reject pride in your life, the more God will use you and your art.

I believe that if we are faithful in giving God the glory, He will be able to trust us with more opportunities, a greater platform, and even more influence in the future. So, practice uncoolness and give God the glory.

Responding to This Material

1. Honestly reflect about who is getting credit for your art.

2. Discuss or reflect on this point: "Every artist who wants to make a radical difference for Jesus needs to come to the point where giving God the glory is non-negotiable even if it means never getting another opportunity again."

3. Discuss or reflect on this point: "The more you are willing to reject pride in your life, the more God will use you and your art."

4. How can you practice "uncoolness" in the scene God has called you to?

5. Memorize and meditate on James 4:6.

PRINCIPLE 4:
No Cross, No Power

> "For I resolved to know nothing while I was with you except Jesus Christ and Him crucified."
>
> 1 Corinthians 2:2
>
> "For the message of the cross is foolishness to those who are perishing, but to us who are being saved it is the power of God."
>
> 1 Corinthians 1:18

PRINCIPLE 4: No Cross, No Power

Many years ago, someone invited me to watch a Christian band play in Sydney, Australia. When they finished their set, the singer spoke. He told the crowd that he had been an alcoholic and had struggled with severe depression for much of his life. But when he came to have a relationship with Jesus, he said his depression disappeared, and so did his addiction to alcohol. And that was the end of the concert.

Now, this man clearly has a wonderful testimony, and Jesus certainly does the things this guy talked about: He can set us free from our addictions, and He can take away depression and alcoholism. All that is true—but that is not the Gospel. In fact, someone who believes in New Age philosophy can stand up and say, "I was depressed, and I was an alcoholic. Then I started to meditate, and now I am not depressed and I'm not an alcoholic anymore." That sort of thing is not unique to Christianity.

Yes, we should tell people about how God changes our lives and sets us free. But what they really need to hear about is the cross. The very core of the Gospel is the death and resurrection of Jesus. Over the years, I have had the chance to lift up the cross in every circumstance imaginable, and time and time again I have seen God move in power when I do. The message of the cross is power, and where there is no cross, there is no power.

That's why Paul said, "When I came to you, brothers, I did not come with eloquence or human wisdom as I proclaimed to you the testimony about God. For I resolved to know nothing while I was with you except Jesus Christ and him crucified." (1 Corinthians 2:1-2). Paul could have spoken about any number of things, but he chose to focus on the cross. I believe he understood that the power of God was in the message of the cross.

So communicating the cross in your art will revolutionize everything, but before communicating the cross, you have to have a deep personal revelation of what it means. Maybe you don't get it anymore. Maybe the cross has become just a cliché to you or a piece of jewelry that you wear around your neck. Today, many people in the church think the cross has become old-fashioned. We want to be modern, so we leave it out in our attempts to be "relevant."

By omitting the cross from our message, we leave out the power of the Gospel. God has chosen to use the foolish message of the cross to shame the wise (1 Corinthians 1:27), which means that if we avoid the cross because of how it will be perceived, we do not really understand what it is or what it means.

So what is the cross?

The cross shows the heart and love of the Father. A love so deep that he was willing to send the most precious thing He had: his son Jesus, only to have him be killed by people who misunderstood and hated him. The cross reveals the only way we can be made clean and shows us that we cannot do it ourselves. It proves how horrific sin and evil actually are. The cross is the basis of all of God's plans. It is why Jesus came.

The cross reveals the passion of Jesus. So many people outside the church today think that Jesus and His followers do not care about injustice, but the cross shows that the opposite is true. It shows how angry God is about suffering and injustice; it proves that He is not passive.

Many non-Christians imagine Jesus as a New Age guru in a white robe walking around with a blank expression on his face. The cross exposes this misconception—Jesus was passionate enough to suffer and die on our behalf.

If you cry out to God and ask him to give you a revelation of the cross so that it is real to you, you can bring that reality into your art. Then boldly take the message of the cross into the secular world and you will begin to see God move in miraculous ways!

One time, my band was invited to play at a church. They asked us if we could do a version of our concert that only included our depiction of the cross and not our full show, and we agreed. A businessman had been invited to see our show by several members of the church. He didn't believe in Jesus and was very cynical about the whole thing. Despite his doubts, he agreed to come.

As he watched our performance, he suddenly couldn't see or hear anything. As we showed Jesus on the cross, his sight came back, but he still couldn't hear and his hands began raising involuntarily. After the show he came up to me, clearly shaken, and asked, "What's happening to me? What's going on?" Although he was surprised, I was not. I explained that he was experiencing the power of God.

I have performed on countless stages in just about any kind of situation you could imagine around the world. The audiences are often cynical and closed to Jesus. The breakthrough always comes when we demonstrate the message of the cross through our show. That is because lifting up the message of the cross unleashes God's power.

Responding to This Material

1. If someone were to ask you what the cross means, how would you respond?

2. Cry out to God and ask him to give you a personal revelation of the cross.

3. Why is it a mistake to leave out the cross in our attempts to be "relevant"?

4. Discuss or reflect on this point: "The breakthrough always comes when we demonstrate the message of the cross. When you lift up the message of the cross, you unleash God's power."

5. Memorize and meditate on 1 Corinthians 1:18–2:5.

"Every generation of Christians has this problem of learning to speak meaningfully to its own age. If we are to communicate the Christian faith effectively, we must know and understand the thought-forms of our generation."

Francis Schaeffer[7]

PRINCIPLE 5:
Be Relevant

> "I have become all things to all men, so that I may by all means save some."
>
> 1 Corinthians 9:22

PRINCIPLE 5: Be Relevant

We have used many different ways to demonstrate the cross over the years. One time, my band was invited to play at the Jaap Edenhall in Amsterdam. The night before, a band played called "Slayer"—an American thrash metal band whose lyrics covered serial killers, Satanism, and warfare. They released albums titled "Haunting the Chapel" and "Hell Awaits." The local newspapers dubbed the events "Heaven and Hell at the Jaap Edenhall."

To illustrate the cross, I was carried on stage in a coffin. While the band was singing about how Jesus defeated the power of death, I came out of the coffin with a white sledgehammer and smashed the coffin to pieces on the stage.

Another time my band strapped me to a cross made out of a microphone stand, attached jumper cables, and electrocuted me.

I am always asking God to give me a more effective way to communicate the cross to a secular audience. The question is, how can we be as relevant as possible to the audience we are trying to reach?

One way I've learned to do this is to "show" people who Jesus is before identifying Him as Jesus. That's because if I were to begin a concert in a secular venue saying, "We are here in the name of Jesus," many people would think, "I know who Jesus is and I'm not interested," and then they would leave.

But the truth is people have all sorts of misconceptions about Jesus. The Jesus they reject, you would likely reject also. Some think He is passive or indifferent. Others may think Jesus exists, but that He is an angry judge keeping a list of all the bad things they've done. Our challenge is to get them to see who Jesus really is.

One way we have attempted to get past these misconceptions is by fusing a theatrical story into our concert that shows the character of Jesus and illustrates his death and resurrection in a modern way. The story is centered on a girl who is seduced by a man and then abused. This intense act reflects the broken world we live in. After the girl is abused, I pick her up, carry her to the front of the stage and cry out to show God's anguish over the pain and suffering of this girl.

Many in the crowd are visibly moved and brought to tears by the scene because they have been abused and destroyed by the world's lies and can identify with the girl in our drama.

At the end of the show, I am killed in the place of this girl. My throat is slit, I am covered in stage blood, and I am thrown in a coffin. Soon after, as smoke fills the stage and the music crescendos, I burst out of the coffin to portray Christ's resurrection. I walk over to the girl and say, "You don't have to listen to lies anymore." I say it again, "You don't have to listen to lies anymore! I died in your place. We can be together again." We embrace, and I say, "You can find your life again." Then I turn to the audience and tell them, too, "You can find your life again!"

The show ends with a speech I give directly to the audience, "The world wants to put you in a cage like a rat. Like a rat on a wheel. I don't want to live in a rat cage. I don't want to die in a rat cage. I'm so sick of the rat cage. Sick of the rat cage lies. Sick of the rat cage jokes. It's time to change the road you're on. It's time to meet the ultimate life force."

Notice the language I use. I don't use overly religious words. Then I say, "It's time to meet the ultimate life force—the One who loved us all along, the One who breaks all the chains. And his name is Jesus."

For over an hour we have shown who Jesus is without identifying Him as Jesus. We've shown that Jesus cares about pain and suffering, and that He is not indifferent. He proved this by taking our place and dying for us.

Since it is not until the end of the show that we identify the main character as Jesus, many people are surprised. "I'm not supposed to like Jesus, but I like Him, and I don't know what to do. I see the truth in this message, and I'm touched."

By showing them Jesus before saying the name of Jesus, a lot of the barriers and misconceptions are avoided, and many people understand for the first time who He really is. At this point, I am able to clearly share the Gospel from the stage and people are almost always open to hearing what I have to say. As a result, I have seen many thousands of people all over the world give their lives to Him when they might never have been open to Jesus in any other way.

Still, there is a tension here that is worth mentioning. While we should strive to relevantly communicate the message of the cross, our attempts to be relevant should never come at the expense of clarity. Nor does it mean we compromise morally or identify with the sins of the scene we are trying to reach. We try to be as relevant as possible so that the Gospel message will be as clear as possible.

Also, being relevant doesn't mean you will avoid being offensive or foolish. Some believe that the reason the Gospel is mocked or rejected is because we have not communicated it relevantly enough. This is not true. The Gospel is confrontational. It is both foolish and offensive.

Paul eagerly worked to communicate in the language of his audience, whether he was speaking to Jews, Greeks, or Romans, and yet he recognized that the Gospel was simply going to be "foolishness" to many. Trying to make the Gospel "cool" is a mistake. Relevance is about clarity, not popularity. If you share the message of the cross—and you must—then there will always be people who dislike the message and reject you.

I always try to be as relevant as possible but never for the purposes of popularity or at the expense of truth. Like Jesus, I simply try to communicate the Gospel relevantly in order to speak the "language" of the people God has called me to reach.

Responding to This Material

1. What misconceptions do people have about Jesus? How can you overcome these misconceptions?

2. Discuss or reflect on this point: "The Jesus they reject, you would reject also."

3. Ask God for new, creative and relevant ways to demonstrate the message of the cross to a secular audience.

4. Discuss or reflect on this point: "Relevance is about clarity, not popularity."

5. Discuss or reflect on this point: "The Gospel is confrontational and will always offend."

PRINCIPLE 6:
Ask For God's Broken Heart

> "I have great sorrow and unceasing anguish in my heart."
>
> Romans 9:2

> "All true passion for Christ comes out of a baptism of anguish."
>
> David Wilkerson[8]

PRINCIPLE 6: Ask For God's Broken Heart

I had been running an evangelistic coffee bar on the edge of Amsterdam's Red Light District and leading street evangelism teams for five years. I was frequently being invited to speak on evangelism, and yet despite all my experience, I felt like God asked me to stop what I was doing and actually get to know the people He was calling me to reach. Why would I need to do that? I was on the streets all the time. After five years, I knew what Amsterdam was all about, right?

I meet a lot of people who want to have an impact for Jesus outside of the church but so often don't know anything about the people God is calling them to.

It is important to understand that knowing the scene has nothing to do with external factors or outward appearances. We can wear all the right clothes and use all the right slogans, but still be completely out of touch with the real culture. It is not about wearing the latest t-shirt or listening to the latest music. That's fashion. As Christian artists, we need to push beyond the surface to connect with the secular scene in a real way.

The incredible thing is that when you take the time to get to know people, God will give you His broken heart for them. Though I had no attraction to punk culture, I knew God wanted to use me to reach them in the early days of my ministry. So I chose to follow God's leading and immersed myself in the punk scene. I went to the clubs, met the people, and found that God began to break my heart for this lost and broken group.

If we don't take the time to get to know the people that God is calling us to, our attempts to reach them will be empty and cold. Let's say you're in a Christian band, and since you know that abortion is a bad thing, you decide to write an anti-abortion song:

"Abortion is bad, it makes God sad..."

The problem is, so often we write songs like this while being completely removed from the pain and out of touch with the reality of the situation. Do you know girls who have wrestled with this issue? Have you let God really break your heart for them? If we haven't cried over the pain, suffering, and guilt of abortion, how can we speak on the issue?

Until I am willing to let God break my heart for the broken people I seek to reach, I cannot write about issues like this with any authority. My message will come off as cold, judgmental, and superficial, and I will give people the wrong idea about God. Our message will be powerless if it is not rooted in a broken heart for the people we are trying to reach.

In my book, Ratcage, I talk about a time when we played in a club called the Bloody Circle of Witches in Brazil, run by two gothic vampires. These two girls wore vampire fangs specially made by a dentist and contact lenses that made them look like demons. The backstage area was decorated with pentagrams and other occult symbols, and before every concert they would ring chimes to invite demons into the club. As we were waiting to play our show, I was very afraid, but soon fear was replaced with calm. I felt this overwhelming sense that Jesus was crying. It was as if His tears were washing over me. I felt like God was saying, "Thank you so much for being willing to go to this club and tell these people that I love them."

During the concert, the presence of Jesus was so strong that people were silent and seemed stunned. Afterwards, I talked with one of the girls with the fangs and contact lenses, and I could feel God's broken heart for her. She looked at me and said, "Maybe I need to think about who Jesus is." So I gave her a Bible. Today, the Bloody Circle of Witches is shut down.

But how have we, in the church today, responded to people and places like the Bloody Circle of Witches? What if the Bloody Circle of Witches moved across the street from your church? Some would say we should march around the club, pray, and engage in spiritual warfare against it; others would organize a petition attempting to ban the club from the neighborhood. No wonder people don't want to follow Jesus if the only experience they have with Christians is combative. It is not "us against them." They are not the enemy; they are the ones Jesus died for. He has a broken heart for them.

You should not feel combative toward the people in the music scene. We fight against spiritual principalities and powers (Ephesians 6:12), not people. God has a broken heart for the people we are trying to reach—whether it is in the clubs or anywhere else. He loves them. We are not fighting against them.

I hate it when I am in clubs and I see Christian bands acting like they are in a battle against the audience or the other bands. Treating the lost as enemies not only fails to communicate the love of Christ, but in fact, drives them farther from it.

That doesn't mean that the people God calls you to reach are always easy to love. Our band had just played a show in one of the most notorious male strip clubs in São Paulo, Brazil. There was hardcore pornography stored in the basement to be distributed to pornographic bookstores. To make room for the audience to watch our show, they had to remove a runway that ran through the center of the theater, which allowed the audience to get closer to the strippers. The guy who organized our concert called himself "Guy." He was about 45 years old, dressed in army fatigues, and was a pretty scary individual. He was constantly trying to corner me before the concert so that he could make crude sexual remarks.

After the concert, I couldn't wait to get out of the club. I had no intention of talking to Guy. I found him revolting and just wanted to get as far away from him as possible. But then I thought, "Okay, I'd better say something nice." So I walked over toward him, planning on saying a quick "thank you" just to be polite so I could leave.

But as I approached him I could feel God's incredible love for him. Instead of a quick goodbye, I passionately shared that Jesus had died for him! As I was saying this, the Holy Spirit fell on both of us like a warm blanket, and Guy started to weep. He showed me matching scars on his stomach and back, where someone had shot him on the street. He said that he had always wondered why he had not died, but that now he understood. And while he said that, I, too, understood something: Guy was someone God loved, no matter how unlovable he seemed to me. Guy was somebody that Jesus died for.

In order for us to reach the lost through our art, we need to know the people God has called us to. We need take the time to really know what is on their hearts. What are they wrestling with? What are the lies they are believing? When I have done this, God has given me a piece of his broken heart and the authority to answer the questions they are really asking. He's allowed me to see the lost through His eyes and share Jesus in a direct, relevant, and loving way. I no longer see the lost as enemies, but as people made in God's image.

Responding to This Material

1. Have you invested the time to really get to know the people God has called you to reach?

2. Have you let God truly break your heart for them? Have you cried over them?

3. Discuss or reflect on this point: "Until I am willing to let God break my heart for the lost, my message will come off as cold, judgmental, and superficial—and I will give people the wrong idea about God."

4. Discuss or reflect on this point: "It is not 'us against them.' They are not the enemy; they are the ones Jesus died for."

5. Ask God to break your heart for the lost, even if they are not easy to love.

"With man this is impossible, but with God all things are possible."

Matthew 19:26

PRINCIPLE 7:
Be Impressed with God, Not the Scene

> "Start getting rid of your own limitations, your own preconceptions and your own repressions. Stop coming to these concerts. Go out into the world and preach the Gospel."
>
> Larry Norman[9]

PRINCIPLE 7: Be Impressed with God, Not the Scene

Over the years, many art scenes have come and gone, along with the limitations and restrictions that go with them. Every genre, every style, and every scene has its 'rules.' They may not be spoken, but they exist. These rules tell you what clothes you can wear, the style of music you can play, how your art should or shouldn't look, and more. I believe as artists and followers of Jesus, we need to be impressed with Him and not the particular scene and its rules.

One rule that transcends every secular art scene is that you don't talk about Jesus—at least not in a way that is clear.

I have had people all over the world tell me, "Being bold for Jesus may have had an impact where you are from, but that won't work here." They'll say, "You don't know these people; they won't respond."

People often think that their circumstances are uniquely difficult. Sadly, the real reason is that they are more impressed with the world than with Jesus. Paul makes this point in his letter to the Galatians (1:10): "Am I now trying to win the approval of human beings, or of God? Or am I trying to please people? If I were still trying to please people, I would not be a servant of Christ."

So ultimately, it is a question of who you are impressed by. If you are impressed by God, there will be no limit to what He can do through you. Specifically, being impressed with God means that you are:

1. **Not limited** by human obstacles
2. **Not limited** by conventional thinking
3. **Taking risks** to share Christ
4. **Changing the scene** and not becoming like the scene

Being impressed with God and not the scene means looking to Him for what's possible. This is incredibly freeing, because the Bible says that with God, nothing is impossible. Do you really believe that?

Many years ago, I was sitting in my apartment in Amsterdam watching a BBC documentary about an underground festival in the Polish city of Jarocin. They were interviewing someone from a band called Moscow, and he was talking about his frustrations with life. He said that he wrote music to express his grief over the injustice in the world. As I was watching footage of thousands of people at the festival, I found myself praying for this band.

As I prayed, I got the feeling that we were supposed to play at this festival. It was a completely ridiculous idea, because we had no invitation, and it was still a Communist country. Nonetheless, I believed that God wanted us to go to that festival.

So I got my band together and we drove a van from Amsterdam to Jarocin, Poland. We had to spend six hours at the border into East Germany, and another six hours to get through the Polish border, so it took us a couple days to get there. When we arrived, they surprised us by saying that we could play on the alternative stage, which had an audience of about 5,000 people.

As we were setting up, an official came up to us and said, "No foreign bands are allowed to play. You have to get off the stage."

A few days before this turn of events, I had talked to a priest in the village. Priests had a lot of political power there, and when we arrived in town I thought we should go to the priest and ask him to bless us. So we had gone to the priest before we did anything else, and I had said, "We want to tell people about Jesus. Would you please bless our band?"

So he did. He prayed over our band and said, "If you want, you can always play in front of our church, and the police can't stop you."

As we were getting kicked out of the festival a couple days later, someone from my band said that I needed to tell the audience what was going on, and at that moment, the priest's offer popped into my mind. So I said to the crowd, "We have just been told that the police are forbidding us to play, but if you want to see us, we are going to be playing in front of the church."

In an instant, we became the forbidden band that everyone wanted to see, and literally thousands of people left the festival to hear us play. We were drawing so many people away from the festival that the organizers invited us to come back and play on the main stage the next day.

During that time, a huge number of people gave their lives to Jesus. At one point, I looked into the audience and saw the singer and the bass player from Moscow—the band I had seen on television back in

Amsterdam. So Jodi and I walked up to them, and I said, "I saw you on television!" They acted a little embarrassed, but I said, "I want you to know that I understand how you feel. I understand how angry you are, but the world isn't going to change through your music. You need to give your lives to Jesus." Both of those guys knelt with me and prayed to ask Jesus into their lives.

Think about how incredible this was. Here I am watching television in Amsterdam, I see a band, I feel like God is asking me to go to this festival in Poland, so I go and end up meeting the band I saw on television and praying with them to receive Jesus. How amazing is that? God can do incredible things if you look to Him for what's possible.

It made no sense to drive to a festival without an invitation and expect to play, but God put it on my heart and I responded. Anyone I would have talked to would have told me that is not how the music scene works. You have to be invited to play. But God is not bound by human rules or obstacles; nothing is impossible for Him. Being impressed with God also means not being limited by conventional wisdom.

A few years ago we were on a tour arranged by a Muslim music agency. We were in Tashkent, Uzbekistan, and I felt like God wanted me to go to the local mosque and give the leaders there some of the Bibles we had. Normal thinking would say that you are not supposed to give Bibles to people in a mosque. But I felt like that was what God wanted, so I went up to them and said, "God has sent me to you, and He wants me to give you these books. They're about Jesus." They took them from me as if they were made of gold and said, "Would you like to come into our mosque and pray?"

I said, "Yes," then took off my shoes, went inside, knelt, and prayed that Jesus would come into the mosque.

Then they asked me, "Can our young people come to your concert?"

And I said, "Yeah, that would be great."

So they told all of their young members to come to our concert, and a large number of Muslims gave their lives to Jesus that night. Many of them were university students who could have a major impact on the city. Conventional wisdom would tell you that what happened in Tashkent was not possible, but we do not follow a God that is bound by our thinking. I know God wanted those men to know the truth. When you are impressed with Jesus and His power, He will do miraculous things in your life that will defy what is possible.

Being impressed with God gives you the freedom to take risks in the way you present the Gospel. It frees you from the rules of the scene.

We were playing at a hardcore punk club in Budapest, Hungary, called "The Black Hole." This place was a classic punk club, and there are certain unwritten rules about what you can do in a punk concert. So even though we were communicating in their "language," the message in our music prompted some aggressive behavior. One guy got on stage with a knife and tried to start a fight. Fortunately, the manager of the band that had played before us swung at his head with a metal folding chair in an attempt to defend me (which I appreciated).

Having lyrics that clearly shared Christ was certainly against the 'rules' of this scene. Yet despite the growing aggression of the crowd, we went a step further. At the end of our concert I said, "Now we want to do a drama for you."

Consider how out of place that was. You do not perform dramas in an underground punk club or any rock venue for that matter. Our drama clearly showed the life, death, and resurrection of Jesus. When the drama was over I said, "If you want to know Jesus, I want you to come and kneel with me now." That kind of statement breaks all the rules, but I said it anyway and called people forward to kneel.

While people in the back were shouting, "Don't listen to him! He's a liar!", many came forward and gave their lives to Jesus.

Afterwards, a guy came up to me and said, "I'm a materialist. I don't believe in God. But when I came to your concert, I felt this spirit. Then when you began speaking, my heart started beating really fast and I wanted to respond, but I was afraid. So I went to the bar, and I started to drink." Then he showed me what he was drinking, as if to prove his story, and continued, "Tell me what I need to do." I put my arm around him, and he gave his life to Jesus.

We were not supposed to be clear with Jesus through our lyrics. We were definitely not supposed to have a drama in a punk club, and yet God moved in power. It's ultimately about reaching the lost for Jesus and not allowing human norms and conventional thinking to confine you as you seek God's guidance on how to do this. Some prevent God from using them in miraculous ways because they are too hung up or aware of what is "possible" in the scene they are called to reach.

I think the problem is too many Christian artists love the scene they are trying to reach. God doesn't call us to love the scene; He calls us to love the people in it. Jesus spoke in the language of the culture He was trying to reach. He ate with people, loved them, healed them, fed them, and used their symbols to communicate who God was, but He never identified with cultural stupidity, confusion, pride, selfishness, injustice, or immorality.

Jesus wasn't afraid to confront culture, because He knew how sick and destructive it was. He healed on the Sabbath, He talked to a Samaritan woman in a public place, He befriended tax collectors, and He ate with immoral people.

Jesus said that He did not belong to the world's system but came to bring another kingdom, and He told his followers that they did not belong to this world either.

This is why I refuse to say that I am a Christian punk, even though I have spent years immersed in punk culture. How unbelievable is it to link Jesus with anything like that—a manmade scene that destroys people! I am a follower of Jesus, not a Christian punk. I am a follower of Jesus, and that is all. I influence the scene, not vice versa.

God wants to use you to challenge the lies in the scene He has called you to reach. In order to do so, you need to be impressed with God and not the scene! Fully understanding that with God nothing is impossible! The same power that raised Christ from the dead is available to all those who believe (Ephesians 1:19-20). When you are impressed with God, you will not be bound by the rules of the scene, by conventional wisdom or human obstacles, and God will do incredible things through your art.

Responding to This Material

1. The Bible says that with God nothing is impossible. Do you really believe that?

2. What limits (perhaps subconsciously) have you put on what God can do in the scene or culture that you are trying to reach? Are you too aware of what is "possible" in the scene?

3. Ask God for a revelation of His power. Memorize and meditate on Ephesians 1:19-20 and consider the amazing promise that the same power that raised Christ from the dead is available to all those who believe.

4. Memorize and meditate on Matthew 19:26 and Galatians 1:10.

PRINCIPLE 8:
What Gives You Authority ON Stage Is What You Do OFF Stage

> "I think we must face the fact that there are differences between those who do and do not follow Jesus, regardless of their culture, chosen art form or profession. If there really isn't any difference in your life and mine a final question must be asked: are you a Christian or simply a poser who likes what he or she gets out of pretending to be what you're really not?"
>
> Glenn Kaiser[10]

PRINCIPLE 8: What Gives You Authority ON Stage Is What You Do OFF Stage

Why does the Christian art scene today have so little authority? Why does it seem so powerless? I think that one of the significant reasons is that people in the scene have compromised.

If you want to be effective in your communication, you need to consider what gives you authority.

One time, a guy in my band went to one of the premier Christian venues in the USA. It is a state-of-the-art facility, and all the big Christian bands play there. He was in the green room and noticed that even though everything else was in perfect condition, the carpet had stains all over it. So he asked the club manager while she showed him around why it was so messed up.

She said, "I'm kind of embarrassed to tell you, but it is because of bands that drink too much and vomit on the carpet.

How unbelievable is that? I am truly shocked by the low standards that many Christian bands have. It is almost beyond belief. They call themselves a "Christian" band, yet that label has no impact on how they live their lives.

2 Timothy 2:20-21 says, "In a large house there are articles not only of gold and silver, but also of wood and clay. Some are for noble purposes and some for ignoble. If a man cleanses himself from the latter, he will be an instrument for noble purposes, made holy, useful to the Master and prepared to do any good work."

As I have said before, I believe God desires that the truth be proclaimed in secular places. He is looking for artists He can use to bring glory to His name. But if I am going to be used in that way, I cannot be a clay vessel. Yes, God loves us the way we are, even though we sin—but He wants us to be gold. He does not even want us to be silver. He wants to do things to glorify His name in our lives, but if we are not willing to deal with sin thoroughly, then He is never going to be able to use us for noble purposes. I believe that too many Christian artists are clay, and Jesus wants them to be gold.

I'll say it again: If you want to have authority in your art, it will not come from what you do on stage; it is what you do off stage that matters.

In my band, I have very strict rules about what I expect in terms of holiness, not because I am legalistic, but because I know that as Christians in a position of public influence, God will hold us to a higher standard (James 3:1).

Many people think that striving for holiness is legalistic. It can be, if your motivation is to get God to love you more or to feel superior to others. However, if your motivation is that you love God and want to see more of His power in your life, then holiness will bring liberation and release.

We need to be willing to let go of our rights because it is not just about us. We have influence over other people, and God wants to be able to trust us not to be a stumbling block to them. Let God purify you, and there will be no limits to how He can use you. I believe that God is looking for people who will accept not only the joy of public influence, but also the responsibilities that go along with it.

For example, when we are rehearsing and on tour, we observe a complete media fast; no television, no movies, no video games and no Internet (aside from necessary communication). I do not think it is a sin to go to a movie or play a video game (depending on the movie or game, of course); I simply do not want anything to distract us or take away our passion for Jesus on tour. So we have a media fast. By the end of a tour, we have often gone for months without watching any movies or television. When I turn the TV on or go online for the first time, I am shocked to realize how trashy and inappropriate it can be. It is as if in our "normal life," we live in a sewer, but we are so desensitized to it that we do not even smell it anymore.

I believe that having high standards also includes not drinking alcohol. People often say to me, "But everybody will think you're weird. I mean, everybody drinks beer. It's part of the culture. You don't want to give them the wrong idea about what it means to be a Christian." But consider the number of people who have friends who are alcoholics or recovering alcoholics, or who have family members who are alcoholics. I can ask a room full of people how many of them have been affected by alcohol, and at least half the room will raise their hands.

This makes me believe that perhaps there is a good reason not to drink if I am in a position of public influence. Do I think it is a sin? No. But does that give me the right to drink when I have an influence on so many, especially when half the people in any given group have been affected by alcoholism? Again, I do not want to make this a legalistic issue. I know very godly people who don't share my conviction, but this is how God has led me. If you seek Him, I believe He will guide you on how to deal with the issue of alcohol in your life and ministry.

The sad truth is that many Christians are simply compromised in the area of alcohol and so cannot be used powerfully by God. As artists, we should be praying, "Jesus, I want to be gold. I don't want any compromise in my life that will mess up your plans or stop you from being able to use me."

We have toured with many secular bands, and it has never been a problem with any of them that we do not drink. Never. They have never looked down on us. We just do not make a big deal out of it. For example, they may ask if we want a beer, and I just say, "Oh, I don't drink." I don't act as if I'm holier than they are. I just don't make a big deal about it. And it has never been a problem.

Interestingly enough, the only people who seem to have a problem with our no-alcohol policy are other Christians. It has never been a problem in the secular world or with the secular artists we work with. In fact, we have more opportunities in secular clubs than we have time for, even in Europe where alcohol is such a huge part of the culture. I cannot even remember all the interviews I've done for magazines, newspapers, and television. Never has abstaining from alcohol limited our opportunities.

And it's not just alcohol. The apostle Paul tells the Ephesians that they should not let any unwholesome talk come out of their mouths, and that obscenity, foolish talk, and coarse joking are out of place (Ephesians 4:29, 5:4). Yet so often, Christians think it's "cool" to swear, as if that makes them radical. In reality, it is compromise, or simple immaturity. Again, when you set high standards, you don't lose credibility with the world, you gain it.

Once, we were invited to play a concert with the band that had opened for Slipknot. Like many bands, they normally use a lot of foul language in their shows. But during the concert when they played with us, the singer did not use any obscenities. I didn't say anything to give him that idea; he just acted out of respect for us. Then, to top it off, the promoter went out of his way to ask if he could get us some juice or soda.

Our standards weren't a problem with the promoter. They weren't a problem with the band. They weren't a problem with anybody. The point here is that compromising doesn't make you relevant, and striving for holiness doesn't limit your opportunities.

I could mention so many other areas, like sexual purity, the kind of websites you visit, and other issues of holiness. But the basic idea is: be as passionate and relevant as possible, but be as pure as possible. That's my motto.

Responding to This Material

1. Are you striving to live a holy life? Are you thoroughly dealing with sin? Or do you call yourself a Christian, but in reality, you are living no differently than the world?

2. Discuss or reflect on this point: "If you want to have authority in your art, it is not what you do on stage; it is what you do off stage that matters."

3. As a Christian artist, are you willing to accept the responsibility of having a position of public influence? If necessary, are you willing to let go of your rights?

4. Memorize and meditate on Psalm 139:23-24. Ask for God's guidance as you strive for holiness, especially in the areas of media (TV, movies, Internet, etc.), alcohol, language, and sexual purity.

5. Discuss or reflect on this point: "Compromising doesn't make you relevant, and striving for holiness doesn't limit your opportunities."

6. Memorize and meditate on 2 Timothy 2:20-21 and James 3:1.

"My piano is not my cross, it is my tool. I'd never play it again if God would show me a more effective tool in my life for proclaiming his Gospel."

Keith Green[11]

PRINCIPLE 9:
Commercial Success Can Be a Sign of Failure

> "I'm only here on Earth to serve God. I never had a career. I don't care about commercialism. I have a ministry and I'll fight for the ministry."
>
> Larry Norman[12]

PRINCIPLE 9: Commercial Success Can Be a Sign of Failure

In the 1980s, there was a Christian band in the United States that became extremely successful. One of their albums went platinum on the secular record charts. But in addition to their significant commercial success, they were also seeing thousands of people come to Jesus each week at their concerts.

Unfortunately, after all this success, their managers started telling them, "Don't talk about God so much in your interviews. Don't be so direct in your lyrics. If you don't talk about God so much, and if your lyrics aren't so blatant, you'll have an even greater platform!" This lie seduced them, and God took his hand off them. I believe their success was due to their willingness to talk boldly about Jesus. Sadly, it's not uncommon for Christian artists to obscure the truth or even omit it entirely in the name of marketability and worldly success.

To be clear, I don't believe it's wrong to make a living as an artist or musician any more than it's wrong for an entrepreneur to run a successful company. There are artists who have the talent, initiative, and good fortune to make money using their gifts, and that's fine. Still, we live in a world where people are constantly lied to. They are lied to by the movies they watch and the music they listen to. Could it be that God would call more musicians and artists to a different calling than everyone else?

I believe God wants to give more bands a big, secular platform whose purpose is sharing the Gospel, not making money. This requires a radical paradigm shift. In No Longer Music, we see ourselves as missionaries first and musicians second. We raise financial support from friends, family, and churches just like any other missionaries. This frees us from having to make decisions based on finances and allows us to focus on the purpose of our band. If you depend financially on having to line up performance engagements, in my experience, eventually you will be forced to choose between "feeding your family" and being bold with the Gospel, and you don't want to find yourself in this position. Free yourself from this predicament by choosing the "missionary," not "professional artist" model.

Using your gifts to share Jesus doesn't mean being indifferent about quality either. In No Longer Music, we strive for artistic excellence, but we simply believe that Jesus, not great music, will open doors. This goes against conventional wisdom. There is a lie that if you are bold for Jesus, you will not have any opportunities to perform outside the church, but we have experienced a different reality.

From day one, we have trusted God for opportunities and have played thousands of concerts and headlined festivals all over the world. After 25 years, the opportunities only continue to increase! By the standards of most bands, we are "living the dream." We travel the world and play music, but I believe these opportunities exist because of our willingness to share Jesus openly and not because of our music or promotion. I believe God continues to use No Longer Music because we have never put commercial success ahead of the Gospel.

That said, I don't believe it's impossible to be clear with the Gospel and be commercially successful. I would love to see a band with a major platform being clear and bold for Jesus, I just think it's very difficult not to be seduced by conventional thinking.

My son Aaron and I traveled to Nashville to meet with a well-known musician who had recently found Jesus. We had made contact with him at a large Christian festival in the U.S. Aaron and I told him and his manager that there was a possibility we could arrange for him to play alongside No Longer Music on the main stage of one of the biggest secular festivals in Europe. It is a crazy festival that attracts over 700,000 people consumed by drugs and alcohol, and they would be eager to listen to him because of who he was in his former band. The promoter of this festival was open to having him come, and he would have had the freedom to bring Jesus to hundreds of thousands of people.

Sadly, his Christian manager told us that they were not interested in being part of such blatant public evangelism because he needed to "protect his client's brand." He argued that if his brand was well managed, he would be positioned to have a "voice" in the music world for years to come. Ultimately, this was an issue of money. By taking this opportunity, his manager knew it would be risking his client's commercial success.

But this is exactly how the world thinks. Music is a business, and a successful business steers clear of controversy and protects its brand. The Gospel is unpalatable and doesn't sell, so we hide it. As followers of Jesus, we are not called to live for ourselves. We were put on this earth to glorify God and tell a lost and broken world that Jesus is the answer.

"Yeah, but I have to provide for my family!" is a response I often hear. Yet Jesus said in Matthew 6:33, "Seek first his kingdom and his righteousness, and all these things will be given to you as well." I can testify from over 25 years of choosing to seek God's kingdom over commercial success that God has provided for my family and me better than I could have provided for myself. It has not always been easy, but God has always provided for our needs.

The fact is, most bands and artists will not be commercially successful. You can have exceptional talent, a winning strategy, and a great work ethic and still never make enough money to support you or your family. I'm not trying to be negative, this is just the reality of the music scene.

I had a friend who was in a successful band. They were signed to a record deal, and they toured constantly. They made tens of thousands of dollars. By most bands' standards they had "made it," and yet after two years of constantly playing shows, the band broke up, still owing their record company several thousand dollars for unsold merchandise.

Sadly, most bands would kill to achieve even a measure of their success, and yet the band ended in financial debt. This is more common than you might think. It seems to me that more bands would want to be freed from this harsh reality.

At the end of the day, when your guitar is collecting dust in the basement, wouldn't there be far more satisfaction in knowing that while you were able to be in a band, you shared Jesus in secular places and didn't just try to "make it"? It seems to me this should be an easy choice for most Christian artists. Don't join the rat race of bands trying to be commercially successful. Do something different. Surrender your gifts to God, ask Him for opportunities, and use the platform God gives you to make an eternal difference. Be bold for Jesus, even if it means sacrificing commercial success.

Responding to This Material

1. Ask God if He is calling you to use your creative talent to share the Gospel rather than pursue commercial success.

2. What are the benefits of choosing the "missionary" versus the "professional artist" financial model?

3. Discuss or reflect on this common lie: "If you are bold for Jesus, you will not have any opportunities to perform outside the church."

4. Discuss or reflect on this point: "Music is a business, and a successful business steers clear of controversy and 'protects its brand.' The Gospel is unpalatable and doesn't sell, so we hide it."

5. Memorize and meditate on Matthew 6:33.

PRINCIPLE 10:
You Must Be Willing to Step Through Fear

> "And do not fear those who kill the body but are unable to kill the soul. But rather fear Him who is able to destroy both soul and body in hell."
>
> Matthew 10:28

> "When I am afraid, I put my trust in you. In God, whose word I praise—in God I trust and am not afraid. What can mere mortals do to me?"
>
> Psalm 56:3-4

PRINCIPLE 10: You Must Be Willing to Step Through Fear

One time, I was invited to speak at a concert held in a warehouse in São Paulo, Brazil. This was not a Christian concert, and the people who came to the warehouse were by no means sympathetic to Christians. So I was thinking, I can't just come on stage and preach. Somehow, I need to get the crowd's attention. Over the years, I have had a penchant for using coffins in ministry, and I thought one might serve me well in this case. So I had a couple guys build a coffin, and we planned for them to carry me onto the stage in the coffin just as the warm-up band was finishing its last song. Then I could jump out and get people's attention, instead of just walking onto the stage.

This seemed like a good plan, but as I was lying in the coffin getting ready to go out on stage, the organizer of the event came in and said, "We need to really pray hard, because the crowd is getting violent. They just beat up a community youth worker outside because their favorite band isn't playing." This wasn't exactly what I wanted to hear, and I was even more nervous because Jodi, my wife, was with me. The audience was so crazy that I was worried for her safety. I told her to stay close to the stage so that I could keep an eye on her.

As I lay in the coffin, waves of fear were rolling over me to the point that my knees were literally shaking. I thought it would look ridiculous for them to carry me out onto the stage with my knees shaking, so I held onto them, hoping they would stop. As the warm-up band finished its last song, the guys carried me out onto the stage in the makeshift coffin. It was so poorly built that I wasn't sure it would hold me and I was worried they would dump me onto the stage.

Despite my fears, the coffin held up, and they set me down in the center of the stage. I gritted my teeth and jumped out of the coffin, which definitely got the crowd's attention. I then told the audience that they didn't have to believe lies anymore, that they were not the result of an accident. I explained that they were created by a father who loved them, and that Jesus had to die in our place so we could be free. Then I invited those who wanted to give their lives to Jesus to respond by coming behind the stage. Many people responded, including one of the policemen who was there to protect us and some of the punks who had beaten up the youth worker out front.

Even the headlining band was touched. As they got on stage to play their set, the singer said, "First of all, I really respect what that guy had to say." He was so moved that I prayed with him later, and our band ended up doing a concert with him the next year.

God moved in power, but first I had to pass the test of fear. I believe God is calling more men and women to an extraordinary life that would have a major impact for His kingdom. Yet every major move of God I have experienced has required me to step through fear. This doesn't mean being reckless, but rather obedient to God's call on my life at any cost.

So how am I supposed to face these impossible situations? What I have learned over the years is that facing fear is not about my strength or bravery, but about my trust in the power of God.

1 Corinthians 2:3-5 says, "I came to you in weakness and fear and with much trembling. My message and my preaching were not with wise and persuasive words, but with a demonstration of the Spirit's power so that your faith might not rest on men's wisdom but on God's power."

Paul was not superhuman. He faced fear to the point of physical trembling. At the same time, he recognized that God's power, not his courage, changed lives, so he was able to be obedient despite his fear. The great news is that being afraid is normal; it's how you respond to the fear that matters.

Recently, my band played in a Turkish city of approximately half a million people with no known Christian church and only a handful of believers. When we got there, we discovered that we were the opening band for the citywide Ramadan festivities (Ramadan is a month long Islamic fast) and that the mayor, other city officials, and a local television station would be in attendance! The tour organizer said that in thirty years of ministry, he had never experienced something like this and he wasn't sure how we should proceed. Some feared that our show could provoke a violent reaction. A very real possibility. I was afraid of what might happen if we were bold, especially considering that my sons Aaron and Ben were part of the team. Some suggested that we not preach afterwards or use the name of Jesus. Just say "God," I was told.

In other tours in Middle Eastern countries, rocks have been thrown at the band, riots have broken out, and we have been threatened and insulted, so I was afraid of what might happen. I went for a walk in the city and cried out to God before the concert, asking for wisdom on how to handle the situation. I knew that this was a test. Would I be willing to step through fear to see the name of Jesus lifted up in this Muslim stronghold? I prayed, "Jesus, I am not going to deny you. Whatever happens is up to you but I refuse to give in to the fear." I asked the rest of band what they thought and they all agreed: we would say the name of Jesus, no matter the consequences.

We found ourselves in a similar situation to that of Shadrach, Meshach, and Abednego in Daniel 3, who refused to deny their faith despite the threat of being burned alive by the King. They boldly declared to the King, "If we are thrown into the blazing furnace, the God we serve is able to deliver us from it, and he will deliver us from Your Majesty's hand. But even if he does not, we want you to know, Your Majesty, that we will not serve your gods or worship the image of gold you have set up" (Daniel 3:17-18).

As the concert started, a television camera crew was getting shots of the show and the crowd's reaction. After demonstrating the message of the cross on stage, I ended the show declaring that Jesus is the answer, and it was translated for all to hear. The reaction from the crowd was unbelievable. We were not attacked as some feared, but instead the crowd was clapping and cheering in spite of the fact that we openly shared the Gospel during Ramadan festivities! We invited those who wanted to know more about our message to sign up for our No Longer Music "Fan Club," which is a Turkish Bible correspondence course. Many people rushed the response table. One hundred and one people signed up, and I was able to give the mayor's son an evangelistic DVD.

The world is desperate to hear the truth. Sadly, the "harvest is plentiful but the workers are few" (Matthew 9:37) and I believe it's largely due to fear. Sharing Jesus openly in secular places isn't easy. You will face fear. Not only the fear of physical harm, but more likely the fear of being mocked, laughed at, slandered, and rejected. If you are willing to trust God and step through fear, He will show up in power, your faith will grow, and you will be able to take on greater challenges in the future. Ultimately, it comes down to trust and obedience. Do we trust God to be who the Bible says He is, and are we willing to obey Him at all cost? If we keep our eyes on Him, we will be able to face fear and see God do incredible things.

Responding to This Material

1. What are your fears as they relate to sharing the Gospel through your art?

2. If being afraid is normal, how should you respond? Consider Paul's example in 1 Corinthians 2:3-5

3. Discuss or reflect on this point: "Every major move of God I have experienced has required me to step through fear."

4. Do you trust God to be who the Bible says He is, and are you willing to obey Him at all cost? Or have you set conditions and limits as to how far you will go?

5. Memorize and meditate on Psalm 56:3-4 and Matthew 10:28.

CONCLUSION:
Revolutionary!

CONCLUSION: Revolutionary!

One day I was listening to the radio, and a well-known Christian band was being interviewed on a popular station. This band had achieved considerable success in the secular music scene. The interviewer asked the singer of the band where he got his inspiration, intentionally setting him up to talk about his faith in God. But instead of taking advantage of this opportunity, he pointed to social issues and life experiences as the inspiration for his music. As he spoke, it was as if I heard a voice saying, "Everyone who denies me here on earth, I will also deny before my Father in heaven." (Matthew 10:33).

How bad will it get before more followers of Jesus speak up? How many people will have to die? How desperate does it have to become? How can we be silent when all people hear are lies?

The hard truth is that being bold for Jesus is a revolutionary calling. You have to be willing to defy not only conventional thinking in the secular world, but often "Christian" thinking as well. You will be mocked, you will be rejected, and it may cost you commercial success. While everyone around you scrambles for opportunities and recognition, you will have to learn to trust God, push through fear, and rely on His power.

But I can attest that this radical call is exceedingly more fulfilling than I could have ever imagined. God has faithfully provided for me and has given me incredible opportunities. He has allowed me to use art not just for making money or gaining recognition, but for an eternal purpose. I have seen thousands of people all over the world radically changed by the power of God, a prize far greater than anything this world could offer!

Author and poet Henry David Thoreau wrote, "The mass of men lead lives of quiet desperation."[13] It is so easy to be seduced into thinking that the world is fine. The reality is the world is a desperate place. People are hungry for something real and eternal.

As followers of Jesus, we have the answer. How can we be silent? Shouldn't we tell people that there is a Savior? If God has given us a platform, do we not have the responsibility to rescue as many people as we can? Don't be like everyone else. Use your art to change the world. Be revolutionary!

SO NOW WHAT?

SO NOW WHAT?

Hopefully, this book has been encouraging and challenging! I believe God wants to do extraordinary things with your life! It's not always easy, but I can attest that God is faithful, and I am extremely grateful that I have His plan for my life and not my own. I know the principles and examples in this book might seem overwhelming, but I can assure you that God has a step-by-step plan for you. You don't need to get there overnight. Seek God and ask Him how He would like you to respond. Whatever you do, don't make a knee-jerk decision. Really ask God for His plan and count the cost. If you will surrender your plans and trust Him, you will experience the revolutionary life you were created for!

To continue digging into this subject, check out our weekly "Provoke&Inspire Podcast", which is designed to provoke and inspire artists to proclaim the revolutionary message of Jesus. It features Chad Johnson, Luke Greenwood, and Ben Pierce along with me, as well as high profile guests from the Christian music industry.

www.comeandlive.com/podcast

Start a Revolutionary Bible Study

As a next step, gather together with your bandmates or other local artists and journey through this book together.

Starting a Revolutionary Bible Study is simple!

1. Make sure everyone has a copy of Revolutionary. It's available in paperback or e-book (See Amazon or www.steiger.org/revolutionary).
2. Meet weekly. If you're in a band, you might meet an hour before your band practice and start out by working through this study.
3. Read a chapter, then read through the questions and the scripture reference. I would encourage you to memorize the scripture reference each week.
4. Discuss how the principle could be applied to your particular context. It's okay to wrestle with the principles and work through different perspectives, as you explore their application.
5. Agree upon and write down goals and next steps to take.
6. Pray together.

Steiger International

Perhaps God is calling some of you to join Steiger International. Steiger is a worldwide mission organization that is called to reach and disciple the Global Youth Culture for Jesus.

This Global Youth Culture is fueled by consumerism, social media, and the entertainment industry. They are watching the same movies, listening to the same music, playing the same video games and influenced by many of the same things.

They are growing up in broken homes and raised on violent movies and pornography. They spend hours online, and look to pop stars and celebrities to guide them. They want something to believe in, but reject any absolute truth. They desire real relationships, but devote hours living in virtual reality. They fight for equality, yet believe in a worldview that reduces them to insignificance. They are continually lied to, which leaves them empty and spiritually vacant.

They are found in every major urban center all over the world and they form one of the largest unreached and influential people groups ever to exist. God's heart breaks for this lost generation.

Steiger raises up missionaries and equips the local church to proclaim the message of Jesus in the language of the Global Youth Culture. It establishes a long-term presence in cities through ongoing outreach, discipleship and local church partnership.

www.steiger.org
www.facebook.com/steigerint
www.instagram.com/steigerinternational
Twitter: @steigerint

Steiger Missions School

For those called to the mission of Steiger, the first step is to attend the Steiger Missions School (SMS), held at the Steiger International Center in Krögis, Germany (near Dresden).

It's a 10-week, intensive training program that gathers people from all over the world with a wide variety of giftings and backgrounds, who feel called to join Steiger's mission to reach and disciple the Global Youth Culture for Jesus.

Throughout the week, there are lectures from experienced frontline missionaries, artists, and church planters from all over the world who understand how to reach the Global Youth Culture. Each student has a personal mentor that they meet with on a weekly basis.

During the 10 weeks, we observe a complete media and internet fast. Sundays are set aside as a day of silence, so that students and staff have the opportunity to seek God in a focused and undistracted way. In a world of constant distraction and noise, the media and internet fast, and the silent day of seeking God are among the highlights of the school for all involved.

Students engage in some of Steiger's frontline missionary work, participating in music and artistic tours and events, going to some of Europe's largest art and music festivals, being part of the local youth scene in European cities.

Upon completion of the SMS, there are numerous opportunities for involvement in Steiger. Many participants are offered internship placements of 3-6 months in the year following the SMS. Those interested in further involvement are encouraged to plan ahead of time, keeping their schedule open for these internship opportunities.

Check out **www.steiger.org/sms** to learn more and apply.

www.facebook.com/steigermissionsschool
www.instagram.com/steigersms
Twitter: @steigersms

Come&Live!

Come&Live! is a ministry of Steiger that is specifically focused on provoking and inspiring artists to proclaim the revolutionary message of Jesus. We are committed to accomplishing this mission by engaging with our artists and the broader community in four strategic areas:

Provoking & Inspiring. Our rallying cry is an appeal for artists to lay down their personal dreams and give everything they have to make Jesus known. Our call is to pursue the lost, boldly proclaiming the name of Jesus through the gift of art.

Training & Equipping. We invest in artists, from the part-time musician to the full-time missionary, preparing and encouraging them to love Jesus and have eternal kingdom impact through their art.

Providing Community. We foster a global community that celebrates and supports artists who embrace this challenging path.

Telling Stories. We give account of what God is doing in and through the lives of our artists, and inspire others to join God's outrageously powerful story of redemption.

See **www.comeandlive.com** to get involved in the Come&Live! Community or to apply to become a Come&Live! Artist.

www.facebook.com/comeandlive
www.instagram.com/comeandlive
Twitter: @comeandlive

FREQUENTLY ASKED QUESTIONS

I run into artists all over the world who are eager to use their gifts to share Jesus outside of the church. Many of them, however, are unsure about how to do this. In this book, I did my best to cover the key principles that will challenge and equip more men and women to use art and music for the purposes of the Gospel. That being said, it's impossible to cover everything.

The following list addresses common questions that I have come across as I've shared these principles in seminars all over the world. I didn't cover them specifically in the text of this book, but I do believe they are worth covering.

Does a band need a leader? Is it possible to have shared leadership?

In my experience, successful bands have a leader and the other band members are humble enough to submit to that person's leadership. They are not democracies. I have never seen a successful band in which everyone voted on everything.

Of course, that does not mean that it is a dictatorship or that the leader does not need input from the other members. The leader desperately needs the input of all the members and for everyone to play his or her role.

God has called some to be leaders and they should not apologize for leading. A good leader leads by influence and inspiration, not by force. On the rare occasion that there is an impasse, the other members should ultimately submit to the leader's decisions.

Submitting to a leader does not keep you from being free; in fact, the opposite is true. When we are willing to be under the leadership that God has appointed—even if the leader is irritating sometimes—it will actually bring more release and more opportunities into our lives, not fewer.

I know people who have amazing musical callings on their lives, but they are not willing to be under authority. As a result, they spend all of their time in their bedrooms playing their instruments, wasting the gifts God has given them.

If you are in a band and there is no designated leader, I suggest that you ask Jesus who is being called to lead. Normally, you will know who it is. If you don't, then the band is probably unhealthy, and perhaps you should split up. If it was God's idea to start the band, He has also called someone to take on the leadership role. Therefore, you need to say, "Okay, God, you have called me to be a part of this band, so I am going to be the leader or support the leader as you see fit." If you can't get behind the structure and vision of the band, you need to leave and find one that you can support, or else start your own band.

Is it okay if a member of my band is spiritually immature or isn't completely in line with the vision of the band?

It is essential that your band members' commitment to Jesus be more important than their art. I believe you shouldn't compromise by taking a good guitarist (or any musician) who doesn't have a strong relationship with God. It is better to have a less skilled guitarist (not bad, but less skilled) who has a passion for Jesus than one who does not. I have seen many Christian bands fail because they compromise by taking someone with great musical talent who lacks the same motivation as the rest of the band. I am sure the same would be true in any form of artistic expression.

I have learned this lesson the hard way, because I have made the wrong decision on more than one occasion. I have compromised on the spiritual side because the guy was a great musician, and rationalized that it was okay. But God did not use our band the way He wanted to until I made things right.

I am not a musician or artist. Do these principles apply to me?

Absolutely! Over the years, art and music have been the primary tools I have used to share Jesus with the lost, but the principles I have learned are for anyone who wants to make a radical difference for God outside of the church. Seeking God, trusting Him for opportunities, not being seduced by the patterns of the world, stepping through fear, as well as the other principles in this book, apply to any Christian regardless of vocation or calling.

Can you invite people to respond in a club when they have paid to be there? Is it always appropriate to have an altar call?

If people have paid to be in a club, I normally do not give an actual altar call from the stage. That doesn't mean I don't give a clear Gospel message; I just offer a less disruptive way for people to respond.

For example, at a large festival in Brazil, I asked the organizer if there was a room where we could talk with people after our show. He told me, "Yeah, the band from France didn't want to sign autographs. You can use the room they were going to use."

So after our concert I said, "If you want to know more about Jesus, we want to talk with you! We have a room available over there where we can talk with you."

The room was packed with people, and we prayed with many of them to receive Jesus. We spent hours in conversations. And it was in no way offensive to the organizers of the festival. They were actually glad that we were there, and they brought us water and whatever else we needed—all while we were talking to people and leading them to Jesus.

When playing at a secular club, ask the organizer if there is a room where you can talk to people after the show, and they will not think anything of it. After the concert, you simply tell people that you want to talk with them and show them where to go. If there is not a room where you can meet, you can take people outside.

If you play an outdoor concert, ask God to make you sensitive to the crowd, and He will show you how to handle it. Sometimes preaching from the stage is the perfect thing to do. Other times, it is better to get off the stage and invite people to follow you to another location.

If the concert has been organized by Christians and is held in a neutral place, then I believe you have a responsibility to preach. Sometimes, instead of staying on the stage, I will jump down and go right to the middle of the craziest, rowdiest people I can find. Then I preach from there.

Should I say 'yes' to every opportunity that is presented to me?

Be eager, and look for opportunities, but do not go ahead of God. God wants to help us, but we have to actually listen to His direction. In 1 Samuel 30:1-2, David and his men were away, and bandits came into their village and captured their wives and children. When the men discovered this (verses 4–6), they wept until they had no more strength in their bodies. They were so angry they started talking about stoning David. Obviously, at this point, David was under great pressure to act, and act quickly. David's own men wanted to kill him and the longer he waited, the greater the chance he would never see his family again.

David was a warrior. He was used to going into battle. He had many great victories in the past, but he didn't take his success for granted. 1 Samuel 30:6-8 says that David found strength in God, and he asked Him, "Shall I pursue this raiding party? Will I overtake them?" In verse 8, God said, "Pursue them.

You will certainly overtake them and succeed in the rescue."

Even though David was under all sorts of pressure to act, even though his own men wanted to kill him, and even though his family was in great danger, he understood that he couldn't move ahead of God.

One time, as we played on the street of a dusty Turkish town on the Syrian border, God moved powerfully. But the next concert we played was the polar opposite in every way. We were on a big, beautiful stage with huge video screens, a high quality P.A. system, and robotic laser lights. Looking around, I thought to myself, maybe tonight will not be too difficult. Before the sound check, some members of the band were in a parade in the city leading people to the stage. Almost a thousand people took surveys from us as they arrived for the concert. The surveys gave them the opportunity to sign up for a Bible correspondence course.

Despite the good turnout, the set-up crew was very unhelpful, and there was a strange "vibe" on the stage and in the audience. At our other concerts people had been very interested in filling out the surveys, but here, whole groups of people started tearing them up. Many stood up angrily and left. Suddenly, thirty police appeared and formed a line facing us. You could feel the tension in the air.

When we reached the part of our concert where we show God's broken heart and I use a song to explain his love to the audience, my translator stopped translating. So I repeated the lyrics again while the band continued to play, but still my translator would not translate.

So while the band played, I went backstage to find out what was happening. I was told that the organizer of the concert was hysterical. "We have the first Christian mayor in the country, and if it is discovered that he invited a Christian band, he could be killed." She was crying and very afraid. I prayed and asked God what to do, and I felt like we should just stop. So we ended the concert abruptly.

A girl from our crew went into the crowd to interview people on camera. "What do you think about our message?" she asked. People became very hostile as they heard her question. "Why are you here?" they demanded. "We are Muslims. Why do you ask such things?" Their response seemed to reveal a mixture of both anger and fear.

The stage crew mocked our translator and told him he deserved to die. "You cannot be a Christian. You are a Muslim, and you should be killed," they said.

Of the 970 people who received surveys only 15 were filled out.

I was stunned, exhausted, and emotionally defeated. We had seen God bring amazing breakthroughs in every concert on that tour in Turkey except this one, where we had the best equipment, the best setup, and the best venue. It didn't make sense. During the 30 hours it took for us to travel to our next location, I started to cry out to God. "Why, God, did you let this happen? We spent all this energy, time, and money to be here. And we put so many people at risk. Why weren't you there with us? You were with us in every other place. Why not this time? We didn't back down, we weren't going to deny you. What happened?"

As I prayed, I felt like God said to me, "David, you never asked me. You assumed that because this opportunity presented itself, it was something you should do."

God reminded me of King David, and how he would always inquire of the Lord before he went into battle. I had forgotten this principle and arrogantly assumed that the battle was ours. I had thought, of course this is something God would want us to do! What a great opportunity! But instead, I should have cried out to Him and asked, "Is the battle ours? Is this a door that you want us to go through?"

It is arrogant to think that I can rush into battle without God. I always need to be careful not to move ahead of him. How much time, energy and resources have I wasted because I didn't inquire of the Lord?

Is it a good idea to tour with a secular band?

If you are in a Christian band, tour with secular bands as much as possible, not just Christian ones. Artists, too, should work alongside non-Christians. Touring with secular bands provides you with a great opportunity to reach them. I have been on many tours with secular bands where one or more of the band members give their lives to Jesus.

Should Christian bands model themselves after secular bands?

Christian artists should not let the world set the standard for what they do. I think many Christian bands make the mistake of just trying to be as good as some other non-Christian band. Influences are unavoidable, but don't confine yourself only to what other artists are doing. Think outside of the box. Don't be scared to try new things. Take risks. Try new, weird ideas. Don't be afraid to be truly original or to do something that has never been done before. Ask God, "What do you want me to do that has never been done before?"

We are supposed to have a relationship with the Creator of the universe, but often Christian artists are the least creative. That does not make any sense. Something is wrong if we just follow secular culture and try to make our creativity imitate the rest of the world. That means that the world sets the standard for what we do instead of God.

Don't just play music. Incorporate all kinds of other artistic expression and effects. You will be amazed at what happens if you dare to take some steps in a new direction and add visual effects to your musical presentation.

What do I do with people after they respond at my concerts?

We cannot forget that we need to take care of people after they make a decision to come to Jesus. Whenever possible, we work with a local church. This makes it easier for the church to develop relationships with the people who come to Jesus during the tour, and connects the new believers with Christians already in the area.

Having a 'meet-the-band' party is a great way to forge a connection with the new believers. Immediately after the concert, announce that you are having a 'meet-the-band' party and hand out flyers inviting people to come. Ideally the meeting should be right after the concert and at a location that is within walking distance. At this party you can continue to build on the relationships you've established at the concert. The relaxed atmosphere of this kind of party allows members of your band to talk one-on-one with people who've responded. In our parties, I often will have one or more of the band members give their testimonies and provide further challenge and encouragement to those who have come.

Another strategy is to invite people to an 'invitation-only' concert after your show; this has been effective in the past. On a particular tour in Brazil, our 'invitation-only' concert was packed with people we had met at previous concerts. Many people gave their hearts to Jesus that night, and since we held the invitation-only concert at a church, they were able to get immediately connected to a body of believers. After one concert, the church added thirty new people to its congregation.

Sometimes, when there is no local church presence, we look at starting churches ourselves. Years ago, we were invited to do a tour in Siberia, and the non-Christian promoter suggested that we start fan clubs that would study the Bible and "other religious propaganda." I thought that was a great idea, so we started fan clubs in eight cities. The fan club leader was actually a pastor, and each club turned into a church. So eight churches were planted in Siberia, all thanks to our non-Christian promoter.

Another option is to have a weekend retreat. After another tour in Brazil, we told people that if they wanted to know more about God, they should come to a camp we were holding after the tour was finished. Huge numbers of people from the clubs came. We had workshops on all the things we do in our show—like fire spinning, how to work a sampler, and playing guitar. Then in the afternoons, I would talk about who Jesus is, why He died, and what God's love is. We saw even more people come to Jesus during that weekend, and those who made decisions during our concerts had a firmer foundation on which to build their faith.

It is essential that we ask God for ways to take care of the people who come to Jesus through our art. When people give their lives to Jesus, it's like they are newborn babies, and newborn babies need to be taken care of or they will die.

About The Author

David Pierce is the founder and executive director of Steiger International. He is a gifted proclamation evangelist, dynamic speaker, artist and visionary.

In the early 1980s, at the height of the European punk rock movement, David Pierce started a Bible study on a barge (called Steiger 14) behind Central Station in Amsterdam, Holland reaching disenfranchised young people of that city. It was there that David started a band called "No Longer Music" (NLM) to use as a tool to communicate the Gospel of Jesus to these young people who would never step foot into a church.

Since then, David has taken the message of Jesus to some of the darkest corners of society, including closed Islamic countries, terrorist clubs, squatter villages, anarchy festivals, brothels, junkie joints, punk & goth music festivals, Satanist clubs and New Age gatherings.

David has seen many thousands find Jesus and his efforts have served as a catalyst for a wave of new ministries, churches and missionaries that have grown into a global, interconnected missions organization called "Steiger International". Steiger is called to reach and disciple the "secularized global youth culture" for Jesus.

In addition, David is committed to bringing powerful teaching to those inside the church. Each year, David preaches in churches, conferences, and colleges all around the world sharing about this bold and cutting-edge ministry and opening opportunities for Christians to more seriously commit their lives to reaching the lost at home and around the world.

David's story is a strong catalyst for action in the Christian community and for the work that God wants to do in the hearts of young people everywhere.

Bibliography

[1] Green, Keith. "Can God Use Rock Music?" Keith Green. www.KeithGreen.com (accessed February 4, 2014).

[2] Kaiser, Glenn. *The Responsibility of the Christian Musician. Giving All to the One Who Gives Freely of the Gift of Creativity*. Chicago: Cornerstone Press Chicago, 1994.

[3] Lewis, C.S. *Mere Christianity*. London: HarperCollins UK, 2012.

[4] Spurgeon, Charles Haddon. *Feathers for Arrows: Or, Illustrations from my Netbook*. Boston: Could & Lincoln, 1870.

[5] This quote was found on Glenn Kaiser's website www.glennkaiser.com which is now taken down. The quotes are used with his personal permission given February 14, 2014 via email.

[6] Green, Keith. "So You Wanna Be A Rock Star". Keith Green. www.KeithGreen.com (accessed February 4, 2014).

[7] Schaeffer, Francis. *Escape from Reason*. Downers Grove: InterVarsity Press, 2006.

[8] Wilkerson, David. "A Call to Anguish". Times Square Church, Media Center.
www.tscnyc.org/media_center.php?pg=sermons&ma=29&sm (accessed February 4, 2014).

[9] Goddard, Steve und Green, Roger. "The tape keeps rolling (Interview with Larry Norman)". www.larrynorman.uk.com/word28.htm (accessed February 4, 2014).

[10] see Nr. 5

[11] Green, Keith. "So You Wanna Be A Rock Star". Keith Green. www.KeithGreen.com (accessed February 4, 2014).

[12] Vink, Jan Willem. "From his hospital bed the veteran talks about rock'n'roll, life and death. (Interview with Larry Norman)". Cross Rhythms Magazine, October 1993.

[13] Thoreau, Henry David. *Walden. Or Life in the Woods*. New York/ London: Sterling Publishing Company, Inc., 2009.

Scripture Index

Books also by David Pierce

Rock Priest
Kingsway Publication (1993)

Ratcage
Steiger Press (2004)

Dancing with Skinheads and Other Bible Study Topics
Steiger Press (1998)

More information about David Pierce:

Websites: www.steiger.org
www.therockpriest.com

Facebook: facebook.com/therockpriest

Twitter: twitter.com/therockpriest

Made in the USA
Lexington, KY
20 July 2017